A First Bible Story Book

Stories retold by

Mary Hoffman

Illustrated by

Julie Downing

For Anna-Louise and William

Editors Marie Greenwood,
Anamita Guha, Kritika Gupta
US editor Rebecca Warren
Designers Rashika Kachroo,
Katie Knutton, Roohi Rais
Managing editor Laura Gilbert
Managing art editors Neha Ahuja Chowdhry,
Diane Peyton Jones
DTP designers Sachin Gupta, Shankar Prasad
Producer, pre-production Nikoleta Parasaki
Producer Srijana Gurung

ORIGINAL EDITION
Editor Lee Simmons
Designer Sheilagh Noble
Managing editor Jane Yorke
Managing art editor Chris Scollen
Producer Josie Alabaster
Religious consultants Rev. Terence Handley McMath,
Donald Kraus, Jenny Nemko
DTP designer Almudena Diaz
Additional design Linda Cole, Mark Haygarth

First American Edition, 2017
Published in the United States by DK Publishing
345 Hudson Street, New York, New York 10014

Copyright © 2017 Dorling Kindersley Limited
DK, a Division of Penguin Random House LLC
17 18 19 20 21 10 9 8 7 6 5 4 3 2 1
001–298701–Feb/2017

A catalog record for this book is available from the Library of Congress.

ISBN 978-1-4654-6334-0

DK books are available at special discounts when purchased in bulk
for sales promotions, premiums, fund-raising, or educational use.
For details, contact: DK Publishing Special Markets,
345 Hudson Street, New York, New York 10014
SpecialSales@dk.com

Printed and bound in China

A WORLD OF IDEAS:
SEE ALL THERE IS TO KNOW
www.dk.com

Contents

Introduction to the Bible

The Bible is a collection of some of the best stories ever told. For hundreds of years they have been familiar to many readers. The stories themselves are full of fascinating characters and exciting incidents and I have tried to tell them in ways that young children can find easy to understand. However, the Bible is different from other story collections. Not all of these retellings are happy, some are sad or even frightening. Therefore you may want to read each of the stories for yourself before reading them aloud. In this way you will be ready for any questions that might arise.

The Old Testament
The Old Testament stories are full of heroes like Noah, Abraham, Moses, and Daniel, who had a special relationship with God. Some, like Jonah, were reluctant heroes and had to be persuaded by strong means.

These stories are also full of vivid pictures—the glorious garden of Creation, the pairs of animals being marshaled into the ark, Joseph's coat of many colors. Some images are disturbing in their power, like Adam and Eve being banished from Eden, the near-sacrifice of Isaac by his father, and the lions who ate Daniel's accusers. But they are as much a part of the Bible as the more comforting imagery of creation, repentance, and salvation.

The New Testament

The imagery of the New Testament is familiar to most of us from Christmas cards and carols and from the Christian symbol of the cross. But the stories themselves are memorable too.

An ordinary Jewish couple suddenly find their lives turned upside down by an angel, who explains that their child will be the son of God. As a baby, Jesus is visited

by important men with rich gifts and a powerful king wants to kill him. As a boy, he amazes people with his wisdom and learning. And as a man, Jesus is a great teacher and performs astonishing miracles, like feeding five thousand people with just five loaves of bread and two fishes.

The New Testament moves from the promise of the first Christmas to its fulfillment in the pain and hope of the Crucifixion and Resurrection. The Easter story is not an easy one for young children, but we owe them the truth about what happened to the man who preached love, peace, and forgiveness. The sorrow of Jesus' death on Good Friday is followed quickly by the joy of his rising from the dead on the first Easter Sunday and this is at the heart of Christian belief.

The Bible begins with Creation and this Bible story collection ends with the Resurrection, both powerful images of fresh starts.

In writing **A First Bible Story Book** I have tried to convey some of the excitement and power of the well-known stories within a framework of hope and reconciliation.

Mary M Hoffman

5

The Old

Testament

God Makes the World

In the very beginning, there was nothing but emptiness, darkness, and lots of water. Then God said the word and the world was filled with light. He had made the first ever Day . . .

. . . but He saw that darknes was good too, so He kept it and called it Night.

On the second day, God divided up the water. He kept some to be the sea. The rest He put up in the sky and made Heaven to keep them apart.

On the third day, God put the seas in their proper places and dry land appeared between them. He told the earth to start growing trees, and grass, and plants.

On the fourth day, He made two big lights to hang in the sky—the sun by day . . .

. . . and the moon by night, and all the stars that keep them company.

On the fifth day, God made all the creatures that live in the water—fishes, whales, dolphins, and octopuses . . .

. . . and then He made all the birds that fly in the air, from the great eagle to the tiny wren.

But the sixth day was the busiest of all. God made all the animals that live on the land, not just the big ones like buffaloes and elephants and tigers, but everything, right down to the smallest beetle.

And finally, He decided to make some people, who would be like Him, a man and a woman, to look after all the animals. God saw that the world He had made was good. On the seventh day He rested.

hat creeps through the grass.

The first man and woman were
Adam and Eve. God gave them a
wonderful garden called Eden. He told
them to eat fruit and plants and take care
of every single living thing in the world. He
told them that every person in the world
would come from them and their children.

But the first job God gave Adam and Eve was to name all the animals. Imagine how hard it would be to choose the right name for the camel, the giraffe . . .

. . . or the ostrich if you didn't know it already!

God visited Adam and Eve in the garden and talked to them. He gave them only one rule. "See that tree over there in the middle of the garden?" He said. "It is the Tree of Knowledge. You must never eat its fruit. If you do, you will die."

Now there was a snake in the garden. It slithered up to Eve and hissed, "Why don't you pick that ripe fruit from the tree in the middle of the garden?"

And Eve said, "God told us not to. If we do, we will die." "Nonsense," said the snake. "God just wants to keep the best fruit for himself."

The fruit looked tasty, so Eve picked one and took a big, juicy bite. It was so good she shared some with Adam. Straightaway, they felt shy and ashamed and realized they had no clothes on.

As soon as God realized they had eaten the forbidden fruit, a sadness as big as the whole world came over Him.

He gave Adam and Eve clothes and sent them out of the garden to raise their children and live without ever seeing Eden again. To make sure, He put an angel with a fiery sword to guard the gate. And all because they had done the one thing He had asked them not to do.

Noah's Ark

Hundreds of years after Adam and Eve, the world had filled up with wicked people. This made God sad. He saw that there was only one good family left on the Earth. They were Noah, his wife, and their three sons Shem, Ham, and Japheth.

God said to Noah, "I am going to send a great flood to wash the Earth clean. Everyone will be drowned except you and your family. You must build a big boat. You'll need space for a lot of food because there will be all the animals to feed."

"Animals?" said Noah. "Yes," said God. "Two of each sort, a male and female, including birds and creepy crawlies— and even snakes."

God told Noah exactly how to build the boat, which was called an ark. All Noah's family had to help, his sons and their wives, because they were all going on the ark too. They painted the wooden ark with sticky tar to keep the water out.

Noah's neighbors thought he was crazy. "A boat!" they laughed. "Haven't you noticed there's no sea around here?" But Noah kept on building.

As soon as the ark was ready, Noah took out his list of animals. His family had been rounding them up for weeks. How the neighbors stared! Two by two, the animals entered the ark.

The bears lumbered, the reindeer pranced, the giraffes swayed, and the snakes slithered.

The elephants were terribly slow, the lions padded behind, t[he] parrots squawked, and the wolves howled. The swift cheetah[s] overtook the crawling crocodiles and leaping kangaroos.

Soon the ark was alive with animals.
It was full of hay, and oats, and food for
the family too. The sky was getting very dark.
"Hurry up!" cried Noah to the waddling penguins.
As the tortoises crept up the gangplank, the first
drops of rain began to fall.

It was as if God had opened a window in heaven and poured
water out. Rain cascaded from the sky, filling all the valleys.
Thunder rumbled and lightning flashes cracked the sky in two.

For 40 days and 40 nights, rain drummed on the roof of
the ark. Then one morning everything was quiet. The rain
had stopped and the sun was shining again.

The people who had laughed at Noah tried to escape the rising floodwater, but only the ark was lifted safely to the top of the swirling water, rising higher than the mountain tops.

The ark drifted for months until it bumped into some rocks. Slowly, the floodwaters sank down and then Noah saw the ark had settled on the high mountain tops of Ararat.

How the animals longed to get off! But Noah wanted to be sure it was safe. Three times he sent a dove out from the ark.

The first time, the dove flew straight back. The second time, it had an olive leaf in its beak. The third time the dove didn't come back at all. It had found somewhere green and fresh to live. So Noah lowered the gangplank and the animals bounded out of the ark.

As the birds flew away, Noah saw a beautiful arch of colors glowing in the sky. It was the first rainbow. God promised that He would never again destroy life on Earth—the rainbow would remind Him of His promise.

Abraham and His Family

After the Flood, Noah's family grew and grew. All the people on the Earth were descended from Noah and his wife. And one of them became very special to God. The man's name was Abraham and his wife was Sarah.

One day, God sent for Abraham and told him that if he went where God led him, he would become the father of a great new nation.

Abraham was puzzled because he and Sarah had no children, but he did as God told him.

Abraham gathered all his people together and, with Sarah and his nephew Lot, set out for Canaan. When they were nearly there, Lot and his people decided to turn to the East . . .

. . . and Abraham and Sarah went to the West.

God spoke to Abraham again, telling him that all the land around him would belong to him and his family. He also said that Sarah would have a son. "Your family will be as many as there are stars in the sky," He said. Abraham was amazed. Surely Sarah was too old to have a child?

Sarah was very surprised to have a baby at last. They called their son Isaac.

But when Isaac was still a little boy, God decided to give Abraham a terrible test. He wanted to see how much Abraham loved Him. God told him to take Isaac up a high mountain and kill him. Abraham was horrified, but he did not tell Sarah what God had said.

He loaded a donkey and took Isaac with him, as if they were just going out for a picnic.

Isaac carried the wood and they set off to climb the mountain.

When they had reached the top, Abraham built an altar and piled wood on top. Isaac thought his father was going to kill a lamb. "Father, where is the lamb?" asked Isaac. "God will provide a lamb," said Abraham, but he could hardly speak for tears.

He set Isaac on the altar and took out his knife. The boy was terrified. Suddenly an angel called out, "Stop! Now God knows how much you love Him. You were ready to give Him your only son." Looking up, Abraham saw a ram in the bushes, which he killed instead of Isaac.

Abraham had passed the test. He hugged Isaac tightly, then took him back home.

Joseph and His Rainbow Coa

When Isaac grew up he married Rebecca and they had twin sons, Esau and Jacob. Jacob, who was also called Israel, settled in Canaan and had a large family. His 12 sons were called . . .

Reuben, Simeon, then Levi and Judah, Issachar and Zebulun,

Gad and Asher, Dan and Naphtali, then Joseph and Benjamin.

Joseph and Benjamin were Jacob's favorite children, but he loved Joseph best of all.

One day Joseph told his brothers about a dream he had had. They were tying up corn in the fields when . . .

. . . all the other brothers' bundles bowed down to Joseph's.

Joseph's dream made his brothers really angry. "Who does he think he is?" they grumbled.

Jacob had given Joseph a beautiful coat, colored like the rainbow, and that made the brothers even more jealous. They hated Joseph so much that some of them wanted to harm him.

So one day while they were working in the fields, they grabbed Joseph and tore his splendid coat off him. They decided to kill Joseph and throw his body into a pit.

But Reuben disagreed and said "Let's just leave him at the bottom of the pit." Reuben secretly meant to come back later and rescue Joseph.

Later, while Reuben was busy, the other brothers sold Joseph to some merchants who were traveling to Egypt.

Then the brothers smeared the rainbow coat with goat's blood and told Jacob his favorite son had been killed by a wild beast.

When the merchants reached Egypt, they sold Joseph to the captain of Pharaoh's guard. Joseph worked hard and after some years he was made head of all the household.

One day, Pharaoh had a nightmare which no-one could explain. Joseph had strange dreams himself and was good at knowing what they meant. So the Pharaoh sent for him.

Pharaoh's dream, seven fat cows came out of the river to graze.

hen seven thin cows followed the fat cows out of the water and
obbled them up. But the thin cows didn't get any fatter.

oseph told Pharaoh that the
ream meant Egypt was going
o have seven years of good
arvests followed by seven
ears of famine.

Pharaoh was so impressed
by Joseph's explanation, he
put him in charge of building
barns to store extra food for the
bad years. And Pharaoh's dream
came true, just as Joseph said.

Years later, during the famine, 11 visitors came from Canaan to ask for food. They were Joseph's brothers. He knew who they were immediately, but they had no idea who this powerful Egyptian was. Joseph decided to test his brothers to see if they had changed.

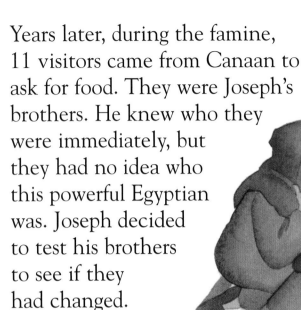

He gave them all the food they could carry, but in Benjamin's sack he hid his special silver cup.

The brothers set off for home, but they had not gone far, when Joseph's guards rode after them and found the cup in Benjamin's sack.

The brothers were arrested and brought to Joseph. He pretended to be angry. "The rest of you can go free," he said, "but the one who stole my cup shall stay and be my slave."

The other brothers were horrified. Their father had already lost one of his favorite sons—it would break his heart if they went back without Benjamin. "Take one of us instead," they begged.

Then Joseph knew they had really changed. He told them who he was and asked them to fetch Jacob so they could all live together in Egypt.

Moses in the Bulrushes

Jacob's family, the Israelites, grew very large. Long after Joseph and his brothers were dead, there were lots of them living in Egypt. The new Pharaoh did not like so many Israelites being in his country.

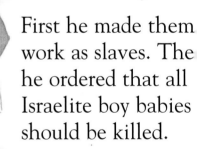

First he made them work as slaves. The he ordered that all Israelite boy babies should be killed.

So Israelite women gave birth i secret. One family decided to save their newborn son in an unusual way. Even th baby's big sister, Miriar was in on the plot.

They kept the baby hidden until he was three months old. By then he was sleeping less and it was harder to keep him a secret.
So his mother wove a basket out of reeds and Miriam helped.

They coated the basket with mud and tar and let it dry. It was like a tiny boat.

The baby's mother put him in his little basket-boat and carried him to the river. She put the basket gently in the water, where it was half-hidden by bulrushes and reeds.

Pharaoh's daughter came down to the river to bathe, as she did at the same time every day. "What is that in the reeds?" she asked. "It looks like a basket."

One of her servants brought the basket to her. "It's a baby!" exclaimed the Princess. "It must be one of the Israelite children. I shall save him and he shall be my son."

ll this time, Miriam had been
ding in the reeds, watching
t for her baby brother. "Your
ighness," she said. "I know an
raelite woman who will nurse
the baby for you."

"Good," said the
Princess. "The baby
must have milk."

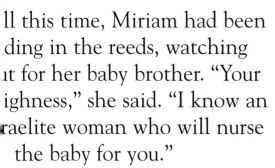

The baby was looked after
by his own mother until he
was old enough to go to
the palace and live with
Pharaoh's family.

The Princess called
the baby Moses,
which means
"taken from
the water."

Daniel in the Lions' Den

The Israelites finally escaped from Egypt. But many years later, they were again made slaves, this time by the Babylonian kings. One of the Israelites who still trusted God was Daniel.

Daniel was so honest and smart that the King, Darius, made him Prime Minister. All the other politicians were jealous.

They made Darius pass a law saying no-one should pray to anyone but the King. Anyone who did would be thrown into a pit with hungry lions.

But Daniel went on praying to God the way he always had. Everyone could see him.

"Daniel prays to God," said the jealous politicians to Darius. "He has broken your law. You must throw him to the lions."

Darius was sad. He liked Daniel, but the law was the law.

He ordered Daniel to be thrown into the lions' den.

Next morning, the King went
sadly to the lions' den, not
daring to hope that Daniel
had been saved.

"Daniel! Has your god kept you safe from the lions?"

"Here I am. God's angel stood between me and the lions."

The King ordered Daniel to be taken out of the pit. He had the politicians thrown in instead and the lions made short work of them, munching on their bones.

Then Darius ordered all his people to respect Daniel's God.

Jonah and the Big Fish

God watched over His Earth and saw that there were still bad things happening on it. He saw that the people of Nineveh were very wicked and violent.
He asked an Israelite teacher, called Jonah, to talk to them.

But Jonah didn't like that idea at all. He didn't want to go to Nineveh.

He ran away from God and got on to a ship that was going to Tarshish, in the other direction.

God knew that Jonah was on the ship and He sent a great storm. All the sailors were terrified.

When Jonah realized what was happening, he told the sailors that the storm was his fault. "I tried to disobey God," he said. "You had better throw me over the side."

The sailors didn't want to do it, but Jonah made them throw him into the water. Immediately the wind dropped and the sea became calm.

45

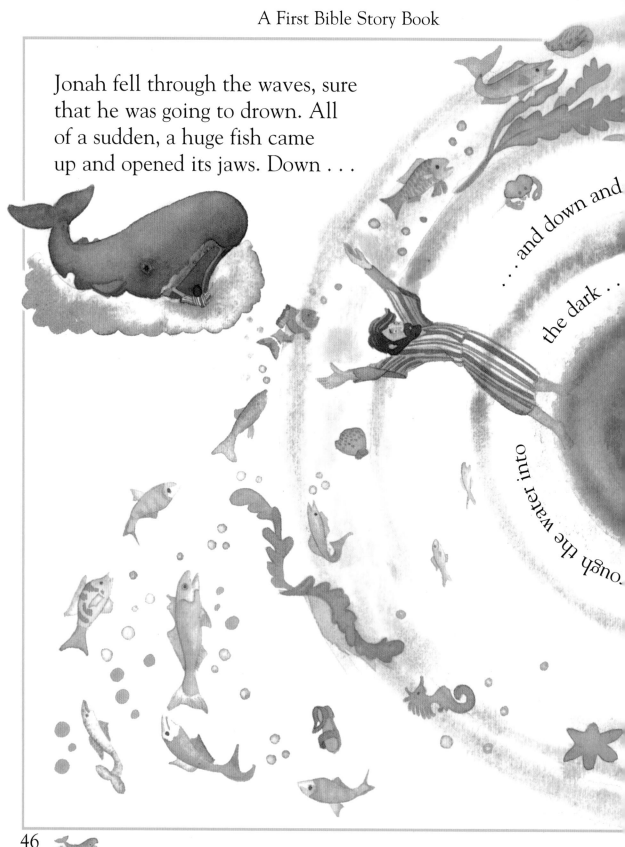

Jonah fell through the waves, sure
that he was going to drown. All
of a sudden, a huge fish came
up and opened its jaws. Down . . .

. . . and down and

the dark . .

ough the water into

wn, and round and round and round went Jonah, swirling and tumbli;

. . . until he ended up inside the fish's belly.

He fell on his knees and prayed to God, thanking Him for saving him from the sea.

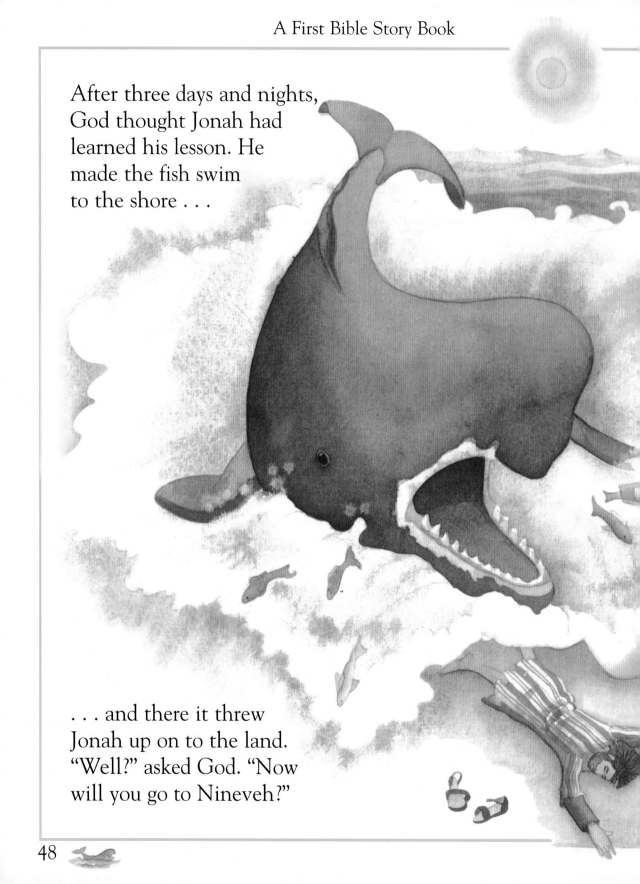

After three days and nights, God thought Jonah had learned his lesson. He made the fish swim to the shore . . .

. . . and there it threw Jonah up on to the land. "Well?" asked God. "Now will you go to Nineveh?"

o Jonah walked all the way to Nineveh.

He warned all
the people that
God would destroy
the city if they
didn't stop doing
bad things.

Everyone, even the King, was sorry. They
all promised to lead better lives in future.
So God did not have to destroy the people
after all. He was glad He could forgive them.

The New

Testament

The First Christmas

When Herod was King of Judaea, there was a good, pure, young woman living in the city of Nazareth in Galilee. Her name was Mary and she was engaged to be married to a man named Joseph.

One day an angel came to Mary and told her she was going to have a baby. "But how?" asked Mary. "I am not married yet."

"This baby will be special. He will be the Son of God."

Mary did not understand, but she agreed to do what God wanted.

fter they were married,
oseph and Mary had to
avel to Bethlehem.
y then it was nearly
me for Mary to
ave her baby.

They searched
everywhere for
a place to stay,
but the city was
crowded. Every inn
was full.

ut one innkeeper
ok pity on them
hen he saw how
red Mary was.
You can sleep in
y stable," he said.

So the Son of God was born
in a stable, where cows
and donkeys were kept.

Mary wrapped the baby Jesus in strips of cloth and put him to bed in a manger filled with fresh hay.

On the hills some shepherds were guarding their
sheep. They were sitting together and dozing
when suddenly the sky was filled with
light and an angel appeared.

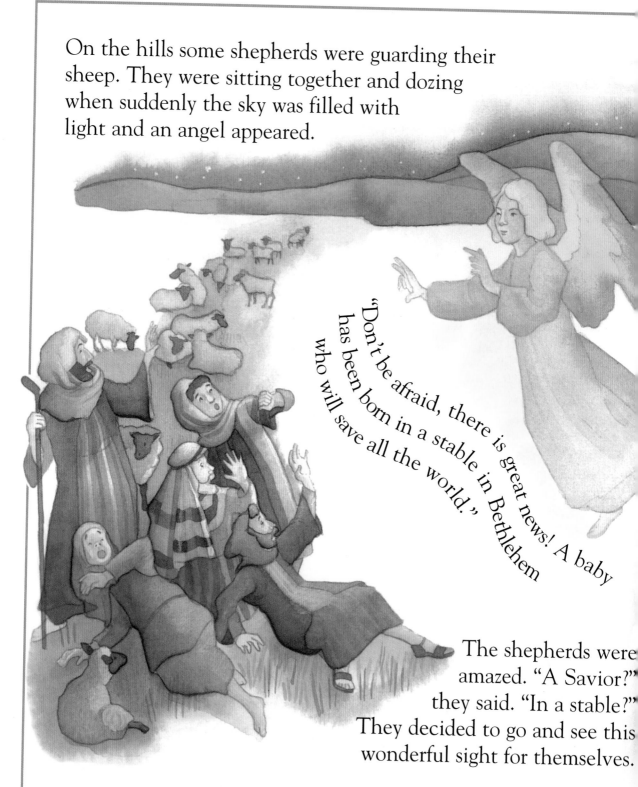

"Don't be afraid, there is great news! A baby has been born in a stable in Bethlehem who will save all the world."

The shepherds were
amazed. "A Savior?"
they said. "In a stable?"
They decided to go and see this
wonderful sight for themselves.

o they took their flocks and
ent down into Bethlehem . . .

. . . straight to the stable where
the baby Jesus was. Later, they
told everyone the amazing
things they had seen and heard.

Mary never forgot that night
and thought about it often.

Three Wise Men

When Jesus was born in Bethlehem, a new star appeared in the sky. Three wise men in the East saw the star and knew a great king had been born.

The three wise men followed the star all the way to Jerusalem.

They went straight to King Herod's palace and asked, "Where is the new king?" Herod was furious, but he pretended to be pleased.

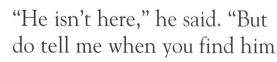

"He isn't here," he said. "But do tell me when you find him

Then the star led the three
wise men from Jerusalem
to Bethlehem and stood
still over the stable.

The three wise men went inside and worshipped the baby Jesus.
They gave him presents of gold, frankincense, and myrrh.

Later, God sent the wise men a dream
that warned them not to see Herod
again. So they went home a different way.

Joseph had a dream too. In his dream an angel came to him.

'You are in danger! You must take Mary and Jesus and run away to Egypt.'

So Joseph and Mary took the baby Jesus and crept out of the stable in the middle of the night.

They set off for Egypt and no-one knew where they had gone.

Herod waited and waited, but the wise men did not return. He flew into a rage. He was King, not this baby.

He ordered his soldiers to kill all the baby boys in Bethlehem, just as Pharaoh had done with the Israelite babies in Egypt in the time of Moses. Jesus had escaped just in time.

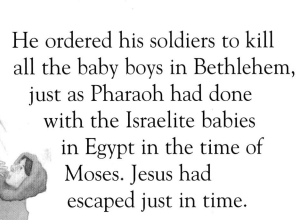

But in the end, the wicked King died and it was safe for Mary and Joseph to bring Jesus back from Egypt.

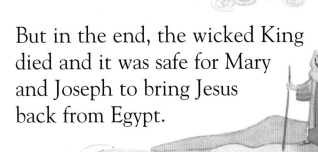

Jesus Is Lost and Found

Jesus grew up happily in Nazareth. Joseph was a carpenter and made furniture in his workshop.

When he was bigger, Jesus helped in the workshop with Joseph.

One day when Jesus was twelve years old, Mary and Joseph took him to Jerusalem for the Feast of the Passover.

When the feast was over, Mary and Joseph set off on the long journey back to Nazareth.

They had lots of friends and relations with them, so that almost a whole day passed before they realized that Jesus wasn't with them. He was lost!

Frantic with worry, Mary and Joseph turned back toward Jerusalem. They searched for Jesus for three whole days. At last, they went sadly to the temple . . .

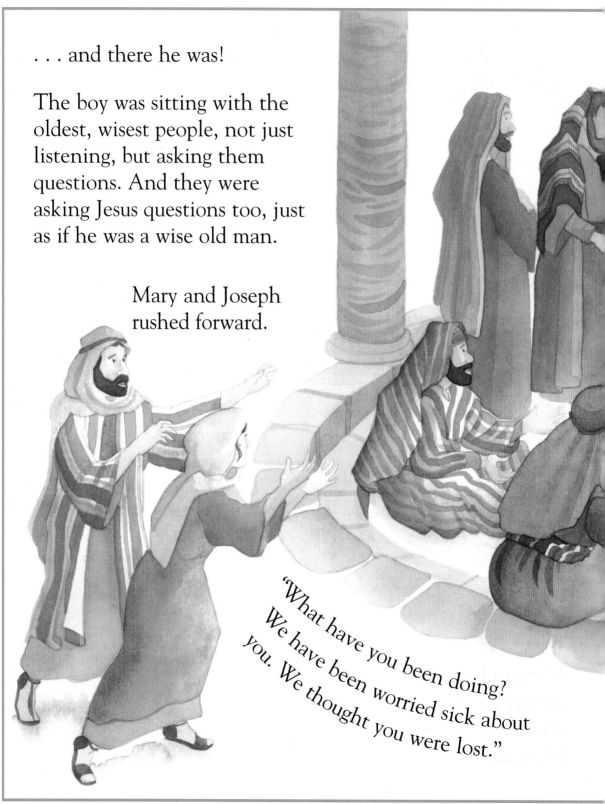

. . . and there he was!

The boy was sitting with the oldest, wisest people, not just listening, but asking them questions. And they were asking Jesus questions too, just as if he was a wise old man.

Mary and Joseph rushed forward.

"What have you been doing? We have been worried sick about you. We thought you were lost."

"You shouldn't have worried. I must do what my Father wants me to do."

Mary and Joseph did not really understand Jesus. Most of the time he was just an ordinary little boy. But Mary never forgot that he was special.

Five Thousand Hungry Peopl

When Jesus grew up, he left his family and traveled all over the country telling people about God.

He chose some friends to join him. They were called his discipl

One day, Jesus was preaching in a deserted place far from any town.

A huge crowd gathered to listen to him and more and more people arrived throughout the day.

y the evening there were about
ve thousand people there and
o-one had anything left to eat.

t is time to send the people
vay," said the disciples.
They must find food."

"Ask if anyone in the crowd has any food," said Jesus.

After a long search, the disciples found a little boy who had just arrived with his picnic. They brought him to Jesus. "This is all we can find," they told him.

Jesus blessed the
food, and told the
disciples to hand
it out.

They looked into the
basket, and saw . . .

two small fishes,

and five barley loaves.

It didn't really look
like enough food
for five thousand people,
but the disciples did as Jesus had asked.

It was astonishing. By the time everyone had eaten as much as they wanted, there were not one, not two, but . . .

one, two, three,

four, five, six,

seven, eight, nine,

ten, eleven, twelve baskets left over.

Imagine how the little boy felt! Everyone began talking about who Jesus could be to make such miracles happen.

The Last Supper

Jesus kept on teaching people about God and it made some powerful people angry. They began to plot against Jesus to see if they could get rid of him.

Then, one Passover, Jesus went to Jerusalem with his disciples.

When everyone was at the supper table, Jesus blessed the bread and the wine.

He gave them to the disciples saying "This is my body and blood which is given for you. Remember me."

Not everyone was pleased to see Jesus.

Some of the disciples went ahead and found a room where they could eat the special Passover meal together.

During the meal, Judas slipped quietly away from the table.

Jesus knew that Judas, one of the twelve disciples, was going to betray him to those people who hated him.

Jesus knew he was going to be killed, so he went to pray in a garden nearby. He asked his disciples to pray with him, but they fell asleep.

Later, Judas came and kissed Jesus. That was a sign for the soldiers, who came forward to arrest Jesus. When the disciples saw the soldiers, they ran away.

esus was taken to Pontius
ilate, the Governor of
idaea. "Are you the King
f the Jews?" asked Pilate.
Yes, it is as you say,"
id Jesus.

Pilate said, "This man has
done nothing wrong. He
should not die." But
the people shouted, "Crucify him!"

Pilate didn't want to be blamed
for Jesus' death, but he chose to
agree with the people's choice.
Jesus was led away to his death.

The First Easter

The soldiers jammed a crown of thorns on Jesus' head and made him carry a wooden cross to a hill outside the city. They made a sign for the cross saying: THE KING OF THE JEWS.

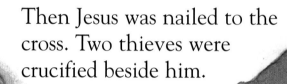

Then Jesus was nailed to the cross. Two thieves were crucified beside him.

Jesus' mother, Mary, and his disciple John stood at the foot of the cross. Jesus asked them to look after one another.

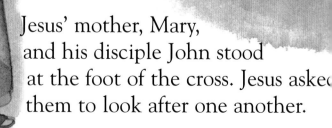

In great pain, Jesus asked God to forgive the people who had plotted to kill him. Then the sky turned black and the ground trembled. Jesus gave a loud cry and died.

One of the soldiers there, who saw all of this happen, said, "Truly, this man was the Son of God."

Jesus' friends gently took his body down from the cross and laid it in a cave. Then they rolled a huge stone across the mouth of the cave.

All the next day, which was Saturday, the Jews' holy day, Jesus' family and friends hid from the soldiers and cried because Jesus had died.

On Sunday morning they went to visit his tomb. But the stone had been rolled back and Jesus' body was gone.

Mary Magdalene, one of Jesus' closest friends, burst into tears at the thought that his body had been stolen. Then Mary saw a man that she thought was the gardener.

But he said to her, "Mary," and she recognized Jesus' voice. Jesus had risen from the dead!

The disciples saw Jesus too, before he joined his Father in Heaven. They told many people about Jesus and God's love. Christians believe that Jesus was sent to die and rise again to save the world.

Who's Who in the Bible Stori

To help you find your way around **A First Bible Story Book**, here
is a list of main characters and the pages where you'll find them.
There's also a reference so you can look them up in the Bible.

Old Testament

Adam and Eve   Page 12
Genesis 1-3
The first man and woman.

Noah   Page 16
Genesis 6-9
The only good man of his
time. God decided to send a
big flood to wash the world
clean of wickedness. Only
Noah, his family, and two of
each animal were saved.

**Shem, Ham,
and Japheth**   Page 16
Genesis 6-9
Noah's three sons.

Abraham   Page 24
Genesis 12-13, 17, 21-22
A descendant of Noah who
had great faith in God. His
son was called Isaac.

Sarah   Page 24
Genesis 12-13, 17, 21-22
Abraham's wife. God gave
her a child when she was
past childbearing age.

Isaac   Page 26
Genesis 21-22
Son of Abraham and Sarah.

Lot   Page
Genesis 13
Abraham's nephew.

Rebecca   Page
Genesis 25
Isaac's wife. They had
twin sons, Esau and Jac

Jacob   Page
Genesis 37, 42-45
The younger son of Isa
and Rebecca. He was
married twice and had
twelve sons. They were
Reuben, Simeon, Levi,
Judah, Issachar, Zebulu
Gad, Asher, Dan,
Naphtali, Joseph,
and Benjamin.

**.eph and
.njamin** Page 28
.nesis 37, 39-45
.ob's two youngest
.ns. Their mother was
.chel, the woman
.ob loved the most.
.eph always looked
.er his little brother
.njamin, even when
.y were grown up.

.araoh Page 32, 36
.nesis 40-41, Exodus 1
.e title given to the
.er of Egypt.

Israelites Page 36
Exodus 1
Descendants of Jacob and
his family.

Miriam Page 36
Exodus 2
Moses' older sister.

Moses Page 36
Exodus 2
An Israelite. Brought up as
an Egyptian, he later became
a leader of the Israelites.

Daniel Page 40
Daniel 6
An important man in
Babylon, whose faith in
God was put to the test.

Darius Page 40
Daniel 6
A ruler in Babylon when
Daniel was alive. He was
a fair king, and was tricked
into sending Daniel to the
lions' den.

Jonah Page 44
Jonah 1-4
An Israelite preacher and a
reluctant hero. When God
asked him to go to Nineveh,
he refused. An adventure
with a large fish changed
his mind.

New Testament

Mary Page 52
Matthew 1-2, Luke 1-2
The mother of Jesus. She was a young girl in Nazareth when an angel told her that her baby would be the Son of God.

Joseph Page 52
Matthew 1-2, Luke 1-2
A carpenter from Nazareth who married Mary.

Jesus Christ Page 54
The New Testament
The Son of God. God loved the world so much, that He sent His son, Jesus, to tell everyone about Him. The whole of the New Testament is about Jesus.

He taught people about the love of God and performed many miracles. Wicked men had him put to death, but he rose again.
   The Christian church was founded to spread his message.

Three wise men Page 58
Matthew 2
Sometimes called the three kings, or Magi. They were men from the East who studied the stars. A new star led them to baby Jesus.

Herod Page 58
Matthew 2
King of Judaea. He was a wicked man, who had all the baby boys in Bethlehem killed when he heard a new king, Jesus, had been born.

Disciples Page
Matthew 14, 26; Mark 6 14; Luke 9, 22; John 6,
Jesus had twelve follow called his Disciples. Th were Simon Peter, And James, John, Philip, Th Bartholomew, Matthew
James, Thadde Simon, and Jud Iscariot

Judas Iscariot Page
Matthew 26, Mark 14, Luke 22, John 13, 18
A disciple; Jesus' betray

John Page
John 19
The disciple who was closest to Jesus.

Pontius Pilate Page
Matthew 27, Mark 15, L 23, John 18-19
Roman governor of Jud

Mary Magdalene Page
Mark 16, John 20
A friend of Jesus. She w the first to see him whe he rose from the dead.